one piano - four ha[nds]

double your fu[n]

EASY
Christmas Duets

by Dan Coates

Dan Coates

As a student at the University of Miami, Dan Coates paid his tuition by playing the piano at south Florida nightclubs and restaurants. One evening in 1975, after Dan had worked his unique brand of magic on the ivories, a stranger from the music field walked up and told him that he should put his inspired piano arrangements down on paper so they could be published.

Dan took the stranger's advice—and the world of music has become much richer as a result. Since that chance encounter long ago, Dan has gone on to achieve international acclaim for his brilliant piano arrangements. His *Big Note, Easy Piano* and *Professional Touch* arrangements have inspired countless piano students and established themselves as classics against which all other works must be measured.

Enjoying an exclusive association with Warner Bros. Publications since 1982, Dan has demonstrated a unique gift for writing arrangements intended for students of every level, from beginner to advanced. Dan never fails to bring a fresh and original approach to his work. Pushing his own creative boundaries with each new manuscript, he writes material that is musically exciting and educationally sound.

From the very beginning of his musical life, Dan has always been eager to seek new challenges. As a five-year-old in Syracuse, New York, he used to sneak into the home of his neighbors to play their piano. Blessed with an amazing ear for music, Dan was able to imitate the melodies of songs he had heard on the radio. Finally, his neighbors convinced his parents to buy Dan his own piano. At that point, there was no stopping his musical development. Dan won a prestigious New York State competition for music composers at the age of 15. Then, after graduating from high school, he toured the world as an arranger and pianist with the group Up With People.

Later, Dan studied piano at the University of Miami with the legendary Ivan Davis, developing his natural abilities to stylize music on the keyboard. Continuing to perform professionally during and after his college years, Dan has played the piano on national television and at the 1984 Summer Olympics in Los Angeles. He has also accompanied recording artists as diverse as Dusty Springfield and Charlotte Rae.

During his long and prolific association with Warner Bros. Publications, Dan has written many award-winning books. He conducts piano workshops worldwide, demonstrating his famous arrangements with a special spark that never fails to inspire students and teachers alike.

BIO01 2/23/04

Contents

FROSTY THE SNOWMAN
Secondo

Words and Music by
STEVE NELSON and JACK ROLLINS
Arranged by DAN COATES

Frosty the Snowman - 6 - 1

FROSTY THE SNOWMAN
Primo

Words and Music by
STEVE NELSON and JACK ROLLINS
Arranged by DAN COATES

Brightly
BOTH HANDS one octave higher throughout

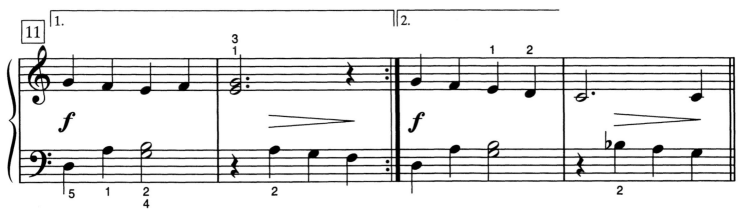

Frosty the Snowman - 6 - 2

Secondo

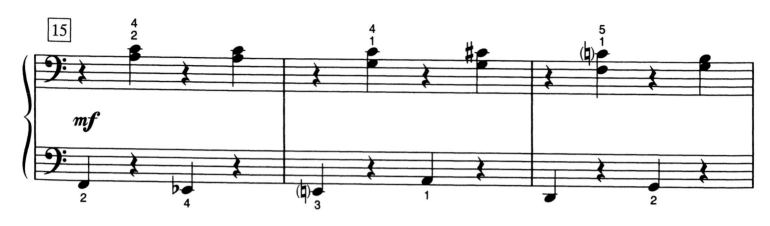

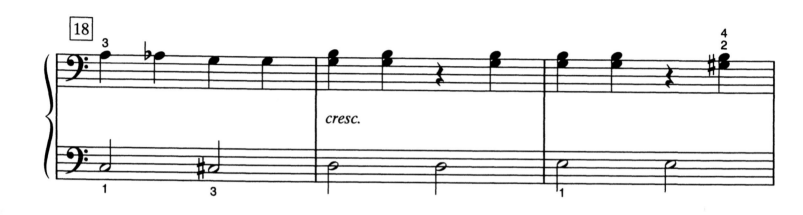

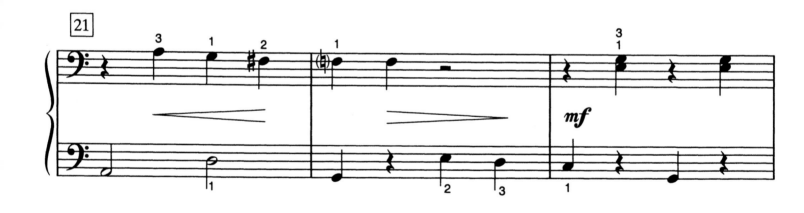

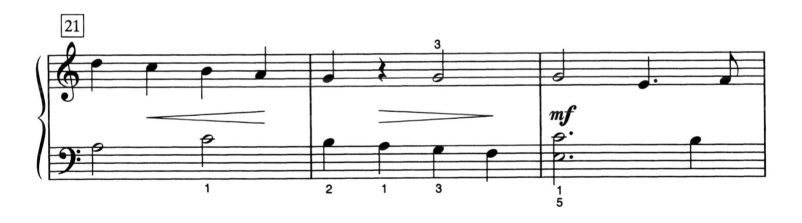

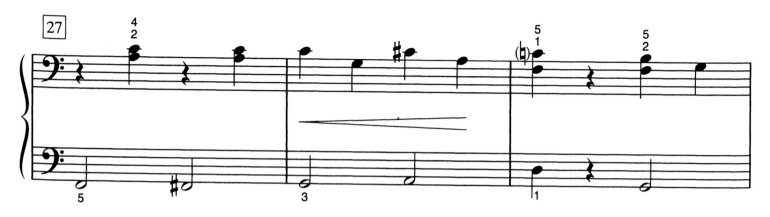

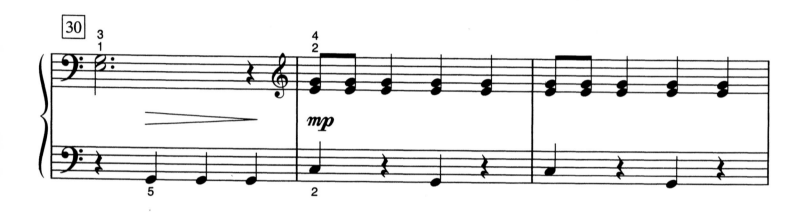

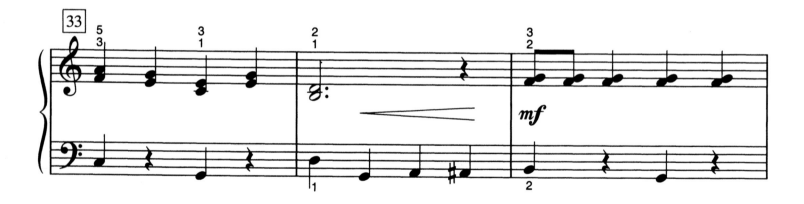

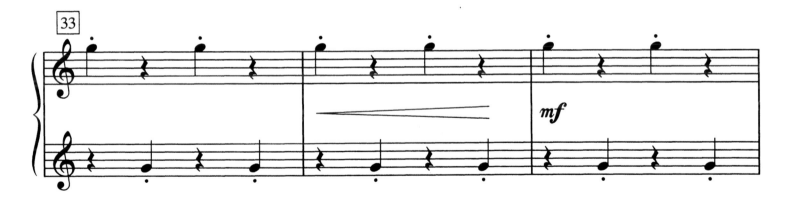

LET IT SNOW! LET IT SNOW! LET IT SNOW!
(Secondo)

Words by
SAMMY CAHN

Music by
JULE STYNE
Arranged by DAN COATES

Moderately, with a swing

Let It Snow! Let It Snow! Let It Snow! - 4 - 1

LET IT SNOW! LET IT SNOW! LET IT SNOW!
(Primo)

Words by
SAMMY CAHN

Music by
JULE STYNE
Arranged by DAN COATES

Let It Snow! Let It Snow! Let It Snow! - 4 - 2

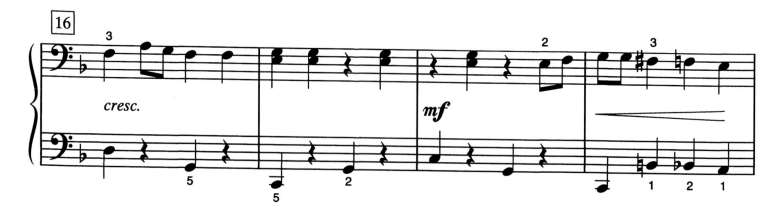

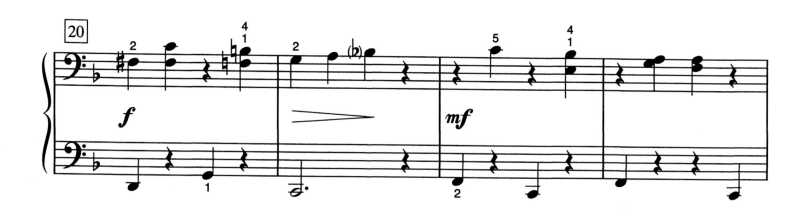

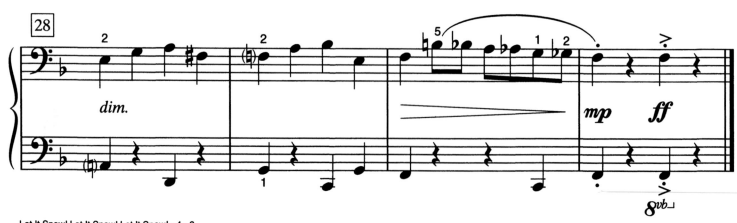

JINGLE BELLS
Secondo

Words and Music by
JAMES PIERPONT
Arranged by DAN COATES

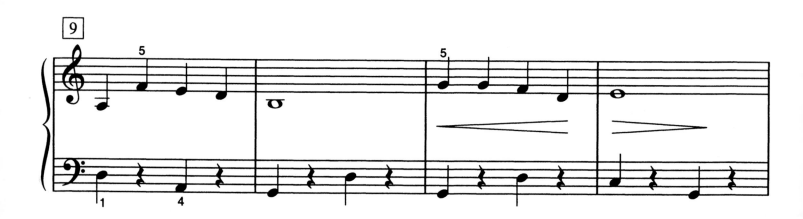

JINGLE BELLS
Primo

Words and Music by
JAMES PIERPONT
Arranged by DAN COATES

Lively

BOTH HANDS one octave higher throughout

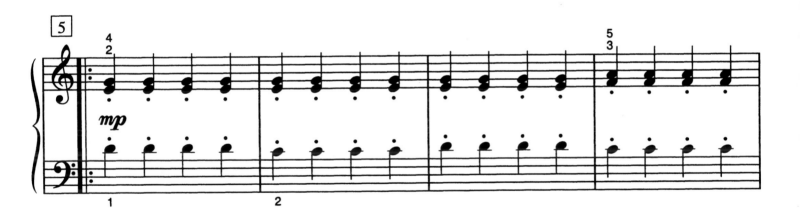

Jingle Bells - 6 - 2

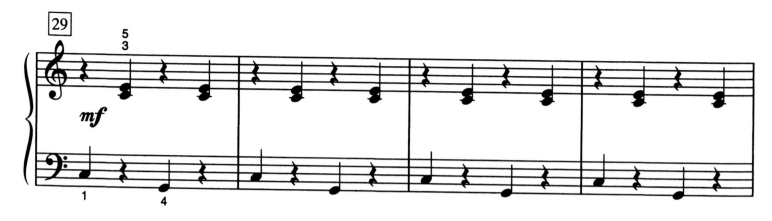

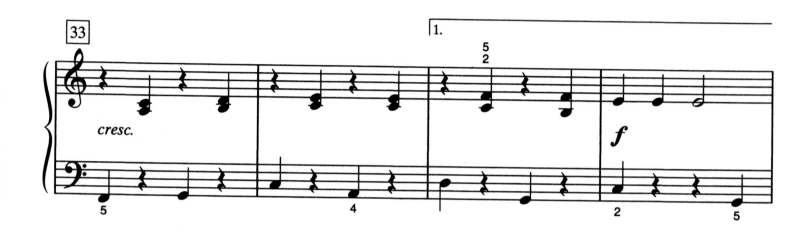

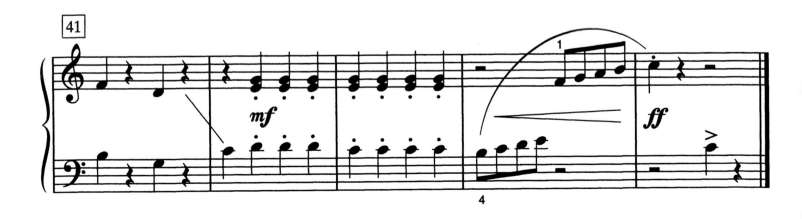

JOY TO THE WORLD
Secondo

Music by
G.F. HANDEL
Arranged by DAN COATES

JOY TO THE WORLD
Primo

Music by
G.F. HANDEL
Arranged by DAN COATES

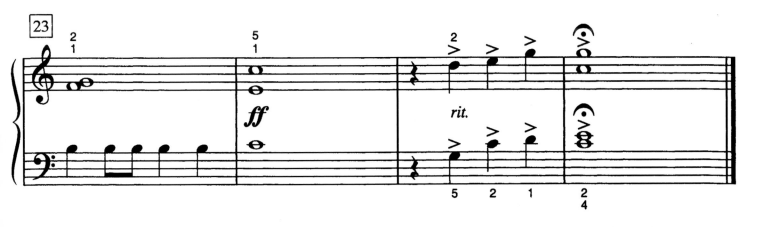

THE LITTLE DRUMMER BOY
Secondo

Words and Music by
KATHERINE DAVIS,
HENRY ONORATI and HARRY SIMEONE
Arranged by DAN COATES

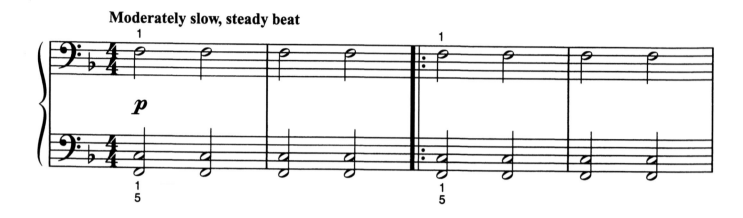

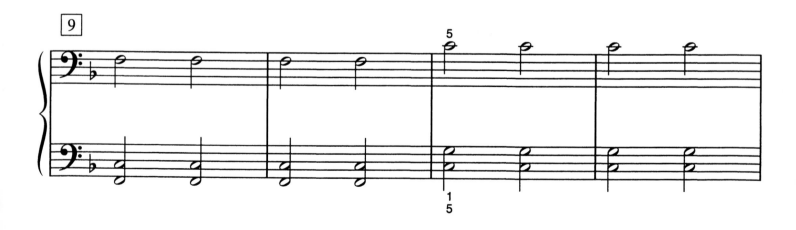

The Little Drummer Boy - 8 - 1

THE LITTLE DRUMMER BOY
Primo

Words and Music by
KATHERINE DAVIS,
HENRY ONORATI and HARRY SIMEONE
Arranged by DAN COATES

Moderately slow, steady beat

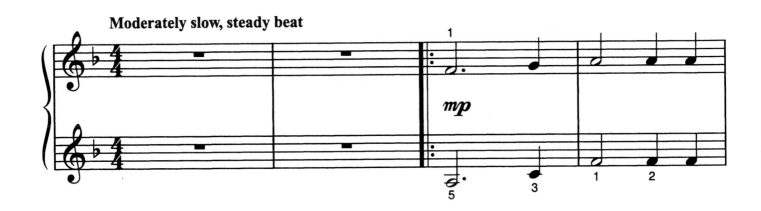

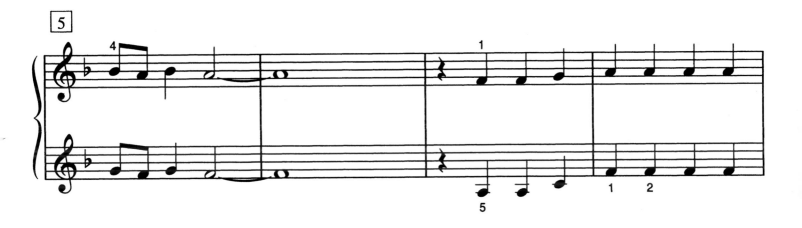

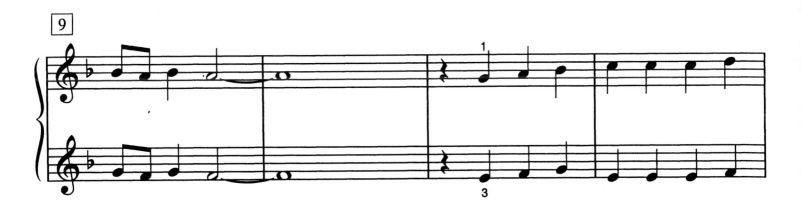

The Little Drummer Boy - 8 - 2

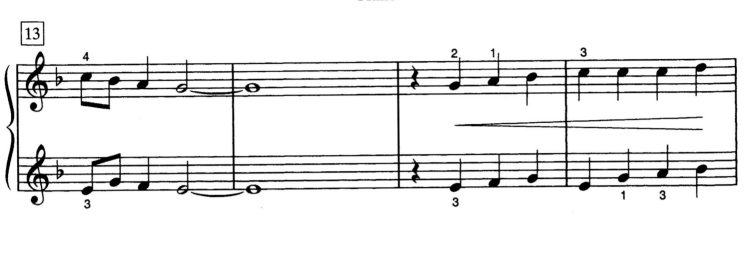

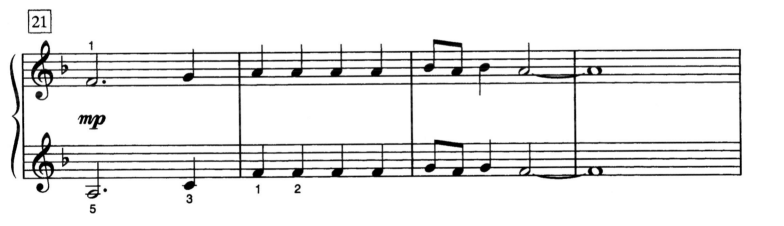

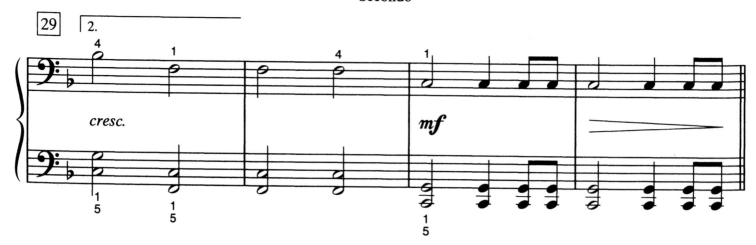

BOTH HANDS *one octave higher through end of piece*

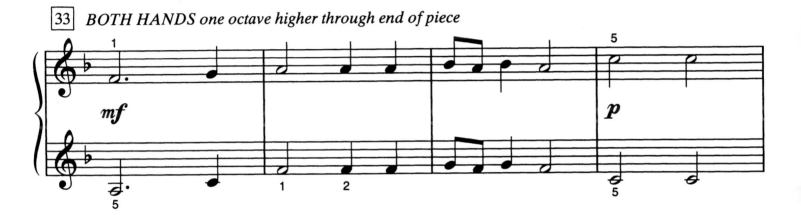

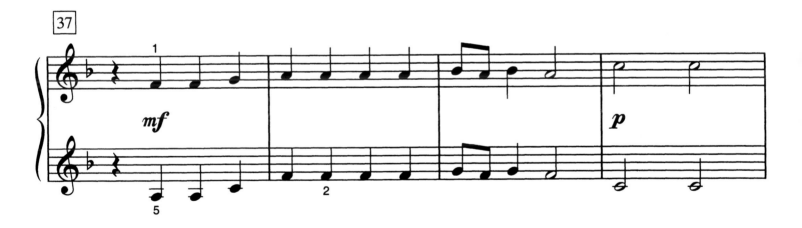

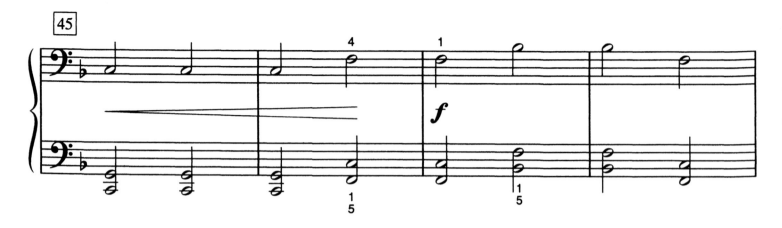

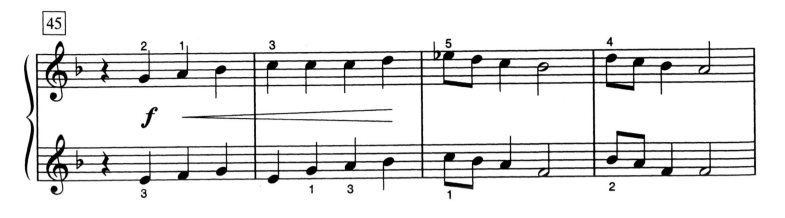

The Little Drummer Boy - 8 - 8

SANTA CLAUS IS COMING TO TOWN
Secondo

Words by HAVEN GILLESPIE
Music by J. FRED COOTS
Arranged by DAN COATES

With a moderate, steady beat

SANTA CLAUS IS COMING TO TOWN
Primo

Words by HAVEN GILLESPIE
Music by J. FRED COOTS
Arranged by DAN COATES

With a moderate, steady beat
BOTH HANDS one octave higher throughout

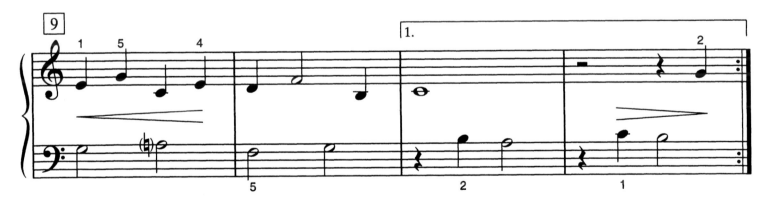

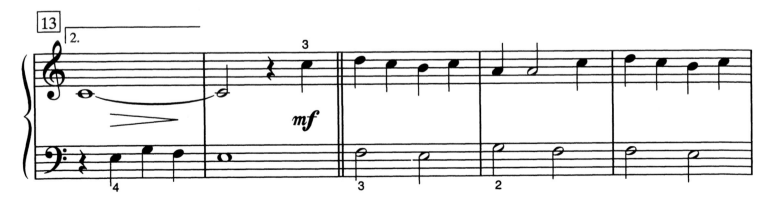

Santa Claus Is Coming to Town - 4 - 2

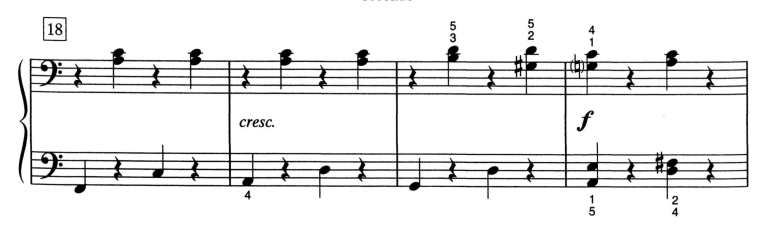

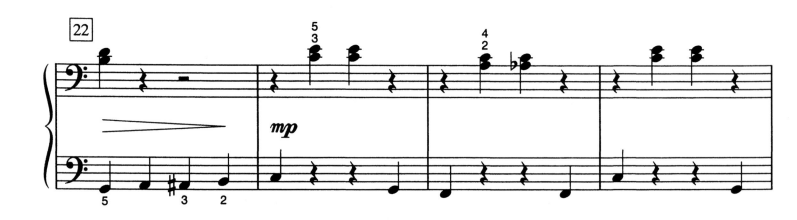

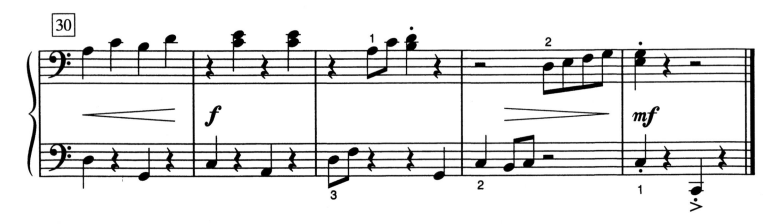

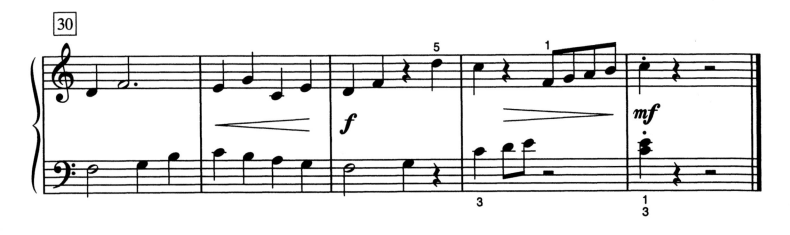

SILENT NIGHT
Secondo

Music by FRANZ GRUBER
Words by JOSEPH MOHR
Arranged by DAN COATES

Silent Night - 4 - 1

SILENT NIGHT
Primo

Music by FRANZ GRUBER
Words by JOSEPH MOHR
Arranged by DAN COATES

Slowly, with expression
BOTH HANDS one octave higher throughout

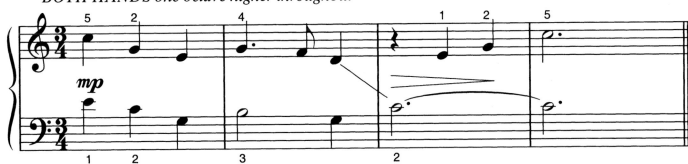

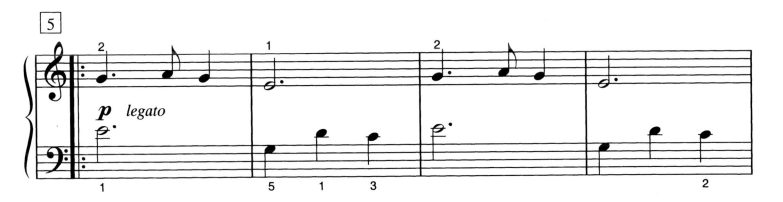

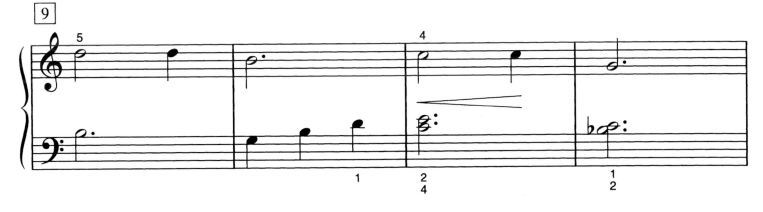

Silent Night - 4 - 2

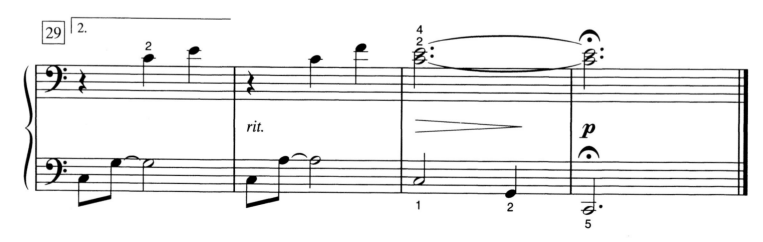

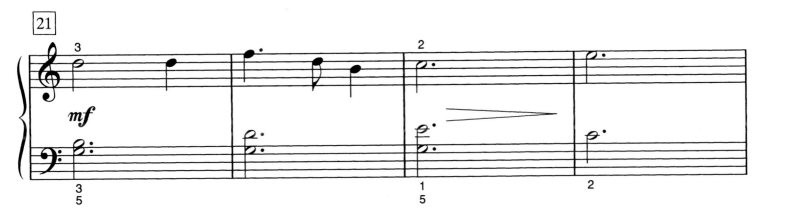

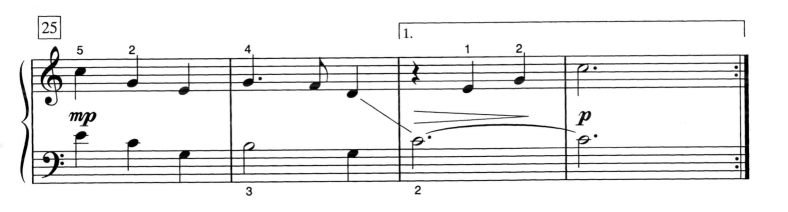

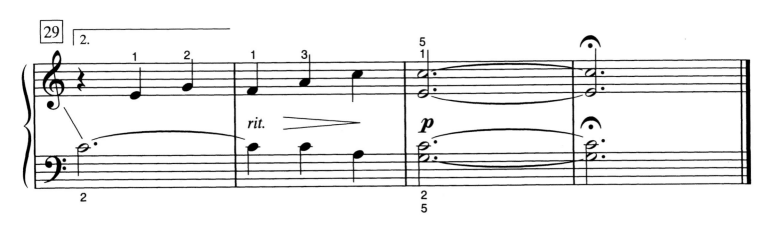

Easy Piano from Dan Coates

2000: The Year in Pop Music

(AFM01015)

Dan Coates adds his expert arranging skills to these top hits of 2000 to make them accessible to the easy-piano-level player while keeping them sounding like the chart-toppers they are.

Titles include: Amazed • Bailamos • Breathe • Genie in a Bottle • Give Me Just One Night (Una Noche) • I Hope You Dance • I Want It That Way • I Will Love Again • Livin' la Vida Loca • Oops!...I Did It Again • Smooth • That's the Way It Is • This I Promise You and many more.

More Pop Hits for the Teen Player

(AFM01005)

Songs from the hottest teen artists such as Backstreet Boys, Britney Spears, Enrique Iglesias, Faith Hill, 98º, ★NSYNC and more. Titles include: Amazed • Beautiful Stranger • Breathe • Give Me Just One Night (Una Noche) • I Still Believe • It's My Life • My Everything • Oops!...I Did It Again • Show Me the Meaning of Being Lonely • Stronger • Thank You for Loving Me and more!

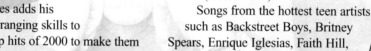

America: The Dream Lives On

(AFM01029)

Seventeen patriotic favorites, including: America • America the Beautiful • America... The Dream Goes On • Anchors Aweigh • God Bless the U.S.A. • The Star-Spangled Banner • This Land Is Your Land • Voices That Care • The Wind Beneath My Wings • The Yankee Doodle Boy • You're a Grand Old Flag and many more.

Smash Pop Hits 2001

(AFM01006)

Titles (and artists) include: American Pie (Madonna) • Babylon (David Gray) • Beautiful Day (U2) • For My Wedding (Don Henley) • I Believe (Andrea Bocelli) • I Turn to You (Christina Aguilera) • Kryptonite (3 Doors Down) • Music (Madonna) • She Bangs (Ricky Martin) • To Love You More (Celine Dion) • WWW.Memory (Alan Jackson) and more!

The James Bond 007 Collection

(AFM01018CD)

Arranged for easy piano by Dan Coates, the *James Bond 007 Collection* contains the main themes of each of the 19 James Bond films. In addition, it features 16 pages of full-color artwork and a fantastic CD with fully orchestrated accompaniment tracks. Titles include: Diamonds Are Forever • The James Bond Theme • For Your Eyes Only • From Russia with Love • Goldfinger • Live and Let Die • The Man with the Golden Gun • Thunderball • Surrender • A View to a Kill • You Only Live Twice and many more.

The Ultimate Pop Sheet Music Collection 2000

(AFM00028)

Dan Coates adds his expert touch to these easy piano arrangements of Warner Bros. Publications' most requested top-selling standards and pop songs. Titles include: Amazed • American Pie • Back at One • Because You Loved Me • Bye Bye Bye • Foolish Games • How Do I Live • I Do (Cherish You) • I Swear • I Want It That Way • Lean on Me • Right Here Waiting • Sometimes • Somewhere Out There and many, many more.